Secret Genealogy VI
Freemasons, Jewish Conquistadors and the Holy Family
by
Suellen Ocean

Secret Genealogy VI
Freemasons, Jewish Conquistadors and the
Holy Family
by
Suellen Ocean
Published by:
Ocean-Hose
P.O. Box 115
Grass Valley, CA 95945
www.oceanhose.com

Also by Suellen Ocean:
Secret Genealogy
Secret Genealogy II
Secret Genealogy III
Secret Genealogy IV
Secret Genealogy V
The Lies of the Lion
The Guild
The Celtic Prince
Black Pansy
Blue Violet
Black Lilac
Ellie
Rose Thorn
Gold River
Gone North
Chimney Fire
Hot Snow
Acorns And Eat'em
Poor Jonny's Cookbook

All rights reserved. No part of this book may be reproduced or transmitted in any form or by any means, electronic or mechanical, including photocopying, recording or by any information storage and retrieval system without written permission from the author, except for the inclusion of brief quotations in a review.

Copyright © January 2017 by Ocean-Hose

Table of Contents

Foreword

Chapter One - *What About Those Stereotypes?*   1

Chapter Two - *What's in a Name?*   6

Chapter Three - *Jewish Conquistadors*   26

Chapter Four – *Origins*   36

Chapter Five - *A Bit About the Brits*   47

Chapter Six - *The Renaissance*   51

Chapter Seven - *Secret Societies, Freemasons, Odd Fellows*   60

Chapter Eight - *The Bible, The Apostles & The Holy Family*   76

Interesting Websites   89

Bibliography   91

Links to Secret Genealogy Series   96

Foreword

Not long ago, I fell asleep and I had a dream. Gray suitcases were lining up on the deck of a 1700's passenger ship. As one by one, the suitcases made their appearance on the deck, a porter stood guarding them. But there was no one to claim them. They were left behind by our ancestors who died long ago. The information in the *Secret Genealogy* books is like those suitcases. I stumbled upon it, like treasures in an attic. I spend a lot of time in that attic, and like priceless antiques, I cannot toss them aside nor leave them for another hundred years. I *love* genealogy. So here is another installment in the *Secret Genealogy* series.

I love history too. And I love the important role that religious history plays in our family trees. This series began with the uncovering of Jewish ancestry from both my mother and father's side. I then began to see and hear Hebrew words, names and ideas throughout American culture. In conversations, books, politics, geography and religion. "Judeo Christian" my husband reminded me but it took a long time to sink in. *Judeo* went in one ear and out the other. Three of the *Secret Genealogy* books share the Jewish theme. This sixth book in the series, returns to that theme because I have more information to share. Or, putting it another way, I have found more "suitcases."

My husband keeps reminding me adamantly that there were many tribes of Israel. The historical truth is, that some of our ancestors may have belonged to one of the twelve tribes of Israel but not to Judah. It would make it easier to understand if it were the **Twelve Tribes of Jacob** instead of the Twelve Tribes of Israel. It isn't correct to call all Semites, Jews. Any more than it would be to label all Arabs, Palestinians. Although it isn't a precise term, "Jews" has taken over as the term for Hebrew tribes. Technically, the Tribe of Judah are the "Jews." Today, "Jews" is also used when speaking of "Israelites."

It must be understood that Jacob is the same person as Israel, which was possibly what he wished to convey. A oneness with God *and* the land. To this day, millions of people have the first name or surname *Jacob*, which might be testament to the man so long ago that with gratitude to God and the land, named himself Israel. The Biblical figure Abraham was the patriarch of the Israelites. Jacob was his grandson and he became prosperous and ruled over a portion of Canaan territory around 1800 B.C.E. The name of the God of the

Israelites was "El Shaddai" or "El." Jacob renamed himself "strength with God," which in ancient Hebrew is "isra-El."

For over 7,000 years there was a Bull Cult religion practiced throughout the ancient world. The Hebrews had other ideas. They came up with monotheism, and brought to the world, the belief in worshipping one god. There was a point in Biblical history, where the Hebrews made a golden calf fashioned after the Egyptian's bull, which may have represented the Bull Cult, but Moses wasn't too happy about seeing the golden calf when he came down the mountain with the Ten Commandments. The rest is history.

Over two-thousand-years ago, tribes from the desert and the hills migrated into Assyria (think Babylon). One of the tribes that came in great numbers was the "Syrian Arameans." This massive tribe spoke Aramaic so it became the predominant language across western Asia. When Jesus came along he spoke it too. Around this time (a couple thousand years ago) there was a "country" called Aram. It was part of Syria. The people who dwelt there were Semitic and called Aramaeans. Their language was Aramaic. But the term Aramaean later came to denote those who were pagan; the Christians took the title of Syrians.

Arabs, Jews, Asians, Africans, Anglos and all other ethnicities have experienced overlapping through the centuries, which is what this book is about; the colorful admixing of our ancestry.

Chapter One

What About Those Stereotypes?

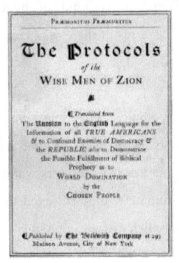

Praemonitus Praemunitus - The Protocols of the Wise Men of Zion - The Beckwith Company (1920)

The book classic *Ivanhoe* by Sir Walter Scott, is a story about medieval England. (It was published in 1820, seven-hundred-and-fifty-four years after the Norman invasion in 1066.) At the end of the story, Ivanhoe, Rebecca and Isaac leave England to begin a new life in Granada. "There under the Moslem law, they hoped to find some measure of peace and security." In the section *about the book*, the following is written:

"The Jewish people were the most wretched, for they were at the mercy of both Saxon and Norman. Christians at this time were forbidden to loan money at interest; so extravagant nobles borrowed from the Jews, sometimes by force, and then hated them because they were in debt to them. Jews suffered every kind of mistreatment, even physical torture. As a result there was contempt, suspicion and violence on both sides."

Contempt between ethnic groups is nothing new. Many of us have hidden Jewish ancestry. Like Rebecca and Isaac in the story "Ivanhoe," our Jewish ancestors wanted to find peace and safety. Unfortunately, they believed that hiding it was their way to accomplish this.

Suspicion against Jews was furthered along in America when in 1903 an anti-Semitic conspiracy theory, *The Protocols of Zion* (The Protocols of the Elders of Zion) was published in Russia. It was a fabricated text of a meeting of Jewish Elders who were supposedly planning for Jewish global domination. It was distributed internationally in many languages. Henry Ford paid for 500,000 copies to be distributed in America. Many believed that it was the authentic text of the minutes of a meeting of Jewish leaders, intent on dominating the world's presses and economies. In 1921, the newspaper, *The Times of London* **debunked** it. But the book is still out there and some still read it and promote it, as if it were true.

In 1922, Hollywood movie studios believed that they needed representation in Washington, so they formed the Motion Picture Producers and Distributors of America. Today it's called, the Motion Picture Association of America. As the politics progressed and Christian organizations protested the indecency of movies, it became necessary for a movie to receive a "Production Code" seal. The man chosen for the job of *chief censor* was an anti-Semite who wrote to a friend that "people whose daily morals would not be tolerated in the toilet of a pest house hold the good jobs out here and wax fat on it. Ninety-five percent of these folks are Jews of an Eastern European lineage. They are, probably, the scum of the scum of the earth."

The German government presented the *The Protocols of Zion* to their students during the Nazi regime. Anti-Semitism left many a Jew offended and frightened about the future. If they hadn't already, wouldn't *some* Jewish parents contemplate hiding the ethnicity of their children to keep them safe? We don't need to ask ourselves what the outcome would be, we know. World War II and Hitler. Some

American Jews tried to hide their heritage by Anglicizing their names, and others were somewhere in the middle. They didn't broadcast their heritage because it brought persecution, ridicule, bad jokes, etc. But most did not abandon it.

In a 2013 article in *The New Yorker*, ("Anti-Semite And Jew," by Anne Applebaum) a man named Csanad Szegedi, the former vice-president of a far-right Hungarian political party with "implied rather than overt" anti-Semitism, resigned from the party after a story broke that his maternal grandmother, now in her nineties, was a survivor of Auschwitz. How ironic.

If you're having a hard time believing that you had Crypto-Jewish ancestry, listen to Applebaum's words. "The Holocaust convinced many European Jews who survived the Second World War that they could never be accepted as equal citizens in their own countries, that they would always be marked in some way. The vast majority of survivors, whether from Hungary, Poland, or Germany, emigrated. But many of those who stayed, especially in Communist Europe, disguised their background, because they were afraid, because they didn't want to stand out, or because they wanted to forget the past and move on."

The rabbi who met with Csanad Szegedi, said that it's not uncommon for Jews in Budapest to discover their ancestry after they grow up. Rabbi Slomo Koves told the author of *The New Yorker* story, that his own "grandmother decided after the war that the main goal of her life was to make all of her children marry non-Jews." (I wonder how she felt that he became a rabbi?) The rabbi's Jewish grandmother was so fearful of what could happen to them because they were Jews, she was "disappointed" that he married a Jewish woman. And Szegedi, the founder of the right-wing Hungarian political party is quoted as saying that his "grandfather thought that for sure there would be deportations again, and there would be a Holocaust again." His belief was that as fast as they could, they had to "assimilate, evaporate, so as to save the family in the future." He probably never dreamed that his grandson would become the leader of a political party with anti-Semitic beliefs, even if they were only "implied."

Chapter Two

What's in a Name?

The name Gabriel reminds us of the association between Christians, Jews and Muslims. In Christianity and Judaism, Gabriel is one of the seven archangels. He is an angel of comfort and a herald declaring the coming of the Messiah. For Islam, Gabriel is believed to have dictated the Koran to their prophet, Mohammed. Christians believe that Gabriel appeared to Mary before she became the mother of Jesus.

As genealogists, we make great leaps into the past. As technology enables the worldwide sharing of our family trees, the more outlandish the claims become. More people come forward claiming that they're the descendants of celebrated historical figures. It sounds outlandish, until you factor in the historical significance of famous people and that their lives were recorded. Who they married, who their parents were, who their children were, their children's' children's' children, etc. is often chronicled.

Authors Patrick Delaforce and Ken Baldry (*The Delaforce Family History Research*) believe that
"Even as late as 1000AD, we have 64,000,000,000 putative ancestors. This figure is about sixteen times the number of people (homo sapiens) who had ever lived before 1800, so we are almost certainly descended from everyone alive in at least Europe & much of the Middle East from that time, let alone the 4th century…"

This kind of open-mindedness is key to finding the truth. If we delve deeply into our genetics, we might find that we're related to most everyone in the world. When the Europeans began exploring North America, stories abounded about how the Native Americans were the lost tribes of Israel. Many people believed that theory. To the minds of sixteenth-century Europeans, it made sense. Generations later, that theory was ridiculed. But in 2013, Jewish news agencies reported that geneticists found a unique Jewish genetic mutation in a Colorado American Indian tribe. The geneticists believe that this particular tribe descends from Inquisitional Jews, who left Spain and fled to the Americas.

This genetic research validates Native Americans who insisted that their ancestors were Jewish.

Because our forefathers and foremothers led us in the opposite direction (they didn't know or didn't want us to know) people are surprised when they discover that they have Jewish ancestry. Our school history lessons didn't exactly teach us about Jews either. I don't believe mine did but I sure got an earful in Christian Sunday school. Today, more and more people are having their DNA tested and are shocked at finding that they have Jewish ancestry. After they recover from the initial shock, they enthusiastically begin to explore Jewish history.

Without resorting to DNA testing, Jewish ancestry can be difficult to prove. I thought my obsession with it had waned. The last *Secret Genealogy* book was about African American ancestry. But here I am, gathering all my research for another installment. I am pleased to report that I found my mother's ancestral name "Bonte" on a list of Jews asked to leave Spain. The name has an "L" next to it, meaning Sephardic/Portugal. The family dates to the 1500's. There were several evolutions of the name... Lueewz, Luiz, Jacob, Jacobse, Jacobi, Bonte and eventually they settled on Banta.

They never settled on a religion. They were supposed to be Dutch Reformed Christians when one of them was arrested for having a Catholic priest baptize his son. To me that was the first red flag after reading that Conversos made "big shows" of their Catholicism. Many of the priests were Conversos who named their children highly-religious names to draw attention away from them. Now I can ask jokingly, does the Spanish government have reparations for me? You will find a link to the list in the chapter, *Interesting Websites.*

The Bonte's were Portuguese Jews, which was my best guess. I just had a hunch. You obviously have hunches too, which is why you are coming back for more *Secret Genealogy*. Addicting, isn't it?

I make leaps when pondering names. I also do a lot of speculating and I ask that you take my speculations into consideration, at the very least it is a lot of fun. I thought the surname "Snow" was weather related. And for some, it may be. But for others, especially the Low Dutch, the word means "small sailing vessel." Snaw, Snauw. I've seen the name Snow on the Dawes list of Indian (Native American) names and thought it referred to the white stuff. Sometimes I'm totally wrong and sometimes I'm absolutely right.

I ran across a trivia question that asked about the Nazis and their requirement that Jews must have Hebrew middle names. The answer was that all Jewish women had to have the middle name of Sarah and Jewish men the middle name of Israel. The Nazis wanted to be able to look at a list and tell by the names whether the people were Jewish or not. Because many Jews have Old Testament Biblical names, the Nazis were content with that. But if a Jew did not have an obviously Jewish name, they were required to add either Sarah or Israel as a middle name. What was particularly interesting was that the trivia answer included the statement "Germans did not have Biblical names, but Americans often do." Let us not forget that Jews living in Germany during the Nazi regime *were Germans* and many of them had Biblical names, long before the Nazis required it.

My husband's name is Jonathan. One day, a German fellow came into his office. When my husband introduced himself as Jon, the fellow said his name was Hans. According to him, "Jon in English is the same name as Hans in German. Hans and Jon," he said, "come from Johann." Wikipedia lists it as the "Germanized form of the originally Hebrew language name, meaning God is merciful."

10

Let's look at another German name. This is an ancient *High German* name. "Luitpold," (also seen as Leudbold). It may link back to the tribe of Judah. "Luitpold," means "people-bold." Liut means "people," and "pold" means "bold." Other versions are Leopold, Leopoldo, Leudbold, Leutpald, Liutbald, Liutpold and Luitpold.

I covered the name Lyon, Lion, etc. in my previous books but I doubt I will ever fail to research this name because it bears such importance for the Jews. The lion is the symbol for the tribe of Judah. When signing documents, ancient Jews could sign either Judah or Lion. This is very important to remember. Leon, Leo, Leopold, Leonardo… these are all variations of Lion or quite possibly their way of saying Judah. Using that name, again and again in its various forms is one of the most prominent clues that say to me… tribe of Judah. Funny how all these years later, many people have a variation of that name and haven't a clue what it means. Of course, there are instances when someone just happens to love that name so gives it to their child. Leon is both a Greek and a Latin name that means lion. But be wise and know how important it was to the Jews. Interestingly enough, Pope Leo was the name of thirteen Roman Catholic Popes. We see leo in Leopold the Great, Leonardo da Vinci, Napoleon and in Winston Leonard Spencer Churchill. If *lee* is a variation of lion, Robert E. Lee, the American general who commanded the Confederates in the Civil War, is also in that list. Whether or not these historical figures, or modern day Germans descend from the lion of the tribe of Judah, would need to be researched on an individual basis.

The language of the Pennsylvania Dutch is a mixture of English and the *High German* from which the name Luitpold stems. Also known as Pennsylvania Germans, these Europeans immigrated from south-western Germany and Switzerland in the 17th and 18th century. In *Secret Genealogy III* (Chapter Nine, Dutch and German Crypto-Jews) I wondered if the ancestors of the Pennsylvania Dutch might have been Crypto-Jews. From the early 1400's, continuing in the early 1800's there was a lot of persecution of Jews. I can see why they would want to emigrate.

There is a lot of history behind a name, including Jews who were stripped of their Hebrew names and given new names. And names that were Anglicized or made to look Celtic with a Mac in front. We can, and should take our surnames apart or be willing to add a prefix or suffix to them to see what the name may have looked like in different countries. For example, take the surname Casper. Change it to a "K" and you have "Kasper." Add the suffix of "sky" and you have a very ethnic sounding name, "Kaspersky."

Quote

The term Ashkenaz is mentioned in the Hebrew Bible in Genesis 10:3 and 1 Chronicles 1:6 as the dwelling place of a descendant of Noah's son Japhet, ancestor of later Europeans. In Jeremiah 51:27 it seems to be part of Asia, perhaps Asia Minor, and is located northwest of Palestine… Although Ashkenaz referred in the Middle Ages only to German lands, the term eventually included northern France and England as well as northern Italy and parts of Central Europe like Bohemia. As Jews migrated into the Polish–Lithuanian Commonwealth, the term broadened to include East European Jews as well.

http://www.yivoencyclopedia.org/article.aspx/Ashkenaz

Ashkenazi – noun for a Yiddish-speaking Jew from Middle, Northern and Eastern Europe (Ashkenazim is plural whereas Ashkenazic is used as the adjective)

If we could, many of us would go back to the beginning of time to uncover our origins. As open-minded genealogists, we want to leave no stone unturned. We seek the truth and will claim *any* ethnicity that belongs on our family tree. In fact, the more eclectic the better, because we know that our ancestry is a colorful trail of paupers, princes, warriors, farmers, queens, silk weavers and who knows what. But how do we know that we *descend* from a particular line? What if your great-great-grandmother was carrying John Smith's baby and she got together with Robert Jones two weeks later and assumed it was his? And who hasn't pondered the question of infidelity? DNA testing might answer some of our questions and prove that our ancestors are truly ours. Until proven otherwise, we're left to accept that all the surnames on our tree belong there.

When I wrote the first *Secret Genealogy* book, I was nervous about what people would say. But I am relieved to say that I have received emails from readers who thank me for sending them in the right direction. One I'm particularly proud of, is the one from a reputable genealogist who said that "... at first I thought you were a total nut case, were tying together many things that I thought total coincidences, but the more I read, the more I looked, the more I now realize that I probably have a whole cluster of families in New Amsterdam… that all were most likely crypto Jewish families that intermarried… I have in recent years discovered MANY Huguenot lines, from both the Flanders and Dutch areas as well as the New Rochelle and Provençal area, which also could have been either Sephardic or Ashkenazi."

I am pleased with this feedback. The Huguenot families are harder for me to decipher. I only have one line that I know of but suffice it to say, he was the leader of a family line that aroused great suspicions. You know the saying… *Methinks the lady doth protest too much.* In this case, it was a man, but his protestations abound in historical records and the things he protested about were what aroused my suspicions.

Quote:
"The immigrant Jew was also made conspicuous by his name. Names like Cohen, Levi or Levy, indicated to the man in the street that the one who bore it was Jewish, even if in all other respects there was nothing to indicate the person's origins. Other names which were commonly borne by German Jews were Aarons, Abrahams, Benjamin, Ezekiel, Isaacs, Israel, Jacobs, Joseph, Mordecai, Moses, Nathan,

Raphael, Samuel and Solomon. These names occurred either as the fore - or surname."

Social Acclimatisation of Jews in 18th and 19th Century Devon, by Reverend Dr Bernard Susser
http://www.jewishgen.org/JCR-uk/susser/acclimatisation.htm

In the very early 1600's, the Dutch East India Company was led by a man named Coen. Although I have never seen it stated that he was Jewish, it is a very Jewish name. During that era, Jews were yet to be accepted in New Amsterdam (New York) and it was a time of persecution for Jews in Holland as well. This Coen, if he was Jewish, would be a perfect example of a "protected" or "court Jew." Here is a recap from the first Secret Genealogy book:

Though you believe your ancestors were Jewish, unless they were "protected" because they were "Court Jews," survival in Germany during the 1600's would have been difficult. Court Jews attained powerful positions of influence in European aristocracy. Whether they were bankers or money managers, consultants or representatives for trade or politics, they rose socially and received its rewards. Though not always permanently, Court Jews lived under noble protection and frequently received titles. Wealthy Jews used intricate networks to keep their sponsors well supplied with commodities and provided loans to Europe's middle class.

Holland is not Germany but it's close. Being the head of the Dutch East India Company was a prestigious position. Coen's job description included supplying commodities to Europeans. And the company was undoubtedly part of the first stock exchange (see *V.O.C.* in the chapter "Secret Societies ... Freemasons, Odd Fellows") that provided investment opportunities to the middle and upper classes. Fascinating to read these names and attach history to them.

I like to take names apart. Like this:
The French name is Deschenes. Separate it, **Des Chenes**. It is a French name and "de" in French means "of." I did a Google search for **Chenes**. Very quickly I find that Chene means oak in French. Les Chene would be "the oak." Some Jews took overtly Christian names to prove that they were true "Conversos," others balked and when forced to change their names, instead of Christian names, they chose the names of plants and bushes. The name "Oak" could be a sign of Jewish ancestry. Or not. Perhaps the family came from a village full of beautiful oaks. But when I Googled "Jewish

Chenes," it brought this quote about Jewish Hellenization before the Christian era. Could the French name Deschenes have originated with a Hellenistic sect in Jerusalem? Or does it just mean "the oak?" There's no end to historical adventures. Amazing.

Quote

"We have mentioned earlier that the king had no intention of abolishing religious diversity, and that neither he nor any other ruler suppressed traditional religious practices when Hellenizing a city or a sect. The Hellenic gods were introduced as early as 173 B.C. when the congregation of "Antio-chenes" was founded in Jerusalem; its members were exempted from observing the Jewish law…" Page 66, The Jewish Expression, Judah Goldin, 1976.

My husband's French-Canadian ancestors have some very long names. One of them is "Marie Madeleine Dupuis Dit Montpellier." It's hard to tell what Marie's surname is. Is it Dupuis or Montpellier? It may be both. "Dit" means that Marie is *called* or *named* Montpellier. But Montpellier is probably **not** the original surname. It could be the name of the region from where Marie originated, it could be her mother's surname or it could be a nickname. Montpellier could be anything. The only thing I know is that Marie is *known as* Montpellier. Her father was Joseph Dupuis Dit Montpellier. A quick Internet search for Montpellier tells me that it is the capital of the Languedoc-Roussillon region of southern France, so I imagine it has a lot to do with that. Paul W. Truax, in his book, "LaForce Descendants in North America," explains that it was a way for New France (Canada) colonists to imitate European nobility by attaching titles to their expansive land grants. It brought prestige when used in business transactions, marriage and baptism records. Truax uses the expression *quasi-nobility* and *self-proclaimed* and his research leads him to believe that these "dit" titles, were viewed with great importance, even more than the original surname, which was often abandoned for the "dit" name. Truax's candidness gives personality to these people who lived in another era.

Quote:

In October 1987 we went to Argentina and visited in Buenos Aires Mula Gdud, the youngest brother of my father-in-law, and his children and grandchildren. Our loving and hospitable family made our visit to this faraway land so cozy... Uncle Mula's reminiscences gave Vova a new slant on the characters of both his father and mother. After this "family get together" we went to the gorgeous Iguasu Falls on the border of Argentina and Brasil. In the hotel dining room there was a big and noisy German speaking table. I usually don't understand German - I have not wanted to listen to the language since 1944 – but their noisy repetition of "Jude, Jude" (Jew, Jew) rivetted my attention. It seems they were saying that Roosevelt was a Jew too. I immediately assumed that these were the Nazis given refuge in Argentina. We ignored them.

"The Memoirs of Samuel Esterowicz." Memoirs translated from Russian and edited by Pearl Esterowicz Good.

Here are some Jewish names that we see throughout the world:

Sam is a very common name. Ever wonder the origins? Samuel is a Hebrew name meaning, "His name is El." El means God, so the name Samuel means, his name is God. Another similar sounding name is Samson or Sampson, also Hebrew and meaning "solar or sun's man."

Joshua is a Hebrew name meaning "the Lord is salvation" or "saviour." Joshua assisted Moses in the wilderness and took over as the leader of the Israelites when Moses died.

Joshua acted as a spy for the Israelites and showed great leadership during the crossing of the River Jordan. Joshua was also a military man who led the Israelite Tribes to Canaan, the "Promised Land." Also pronounced Jehoshua, Jehoshuah and Oshea. In the Greek form, Joshua is the same name as Jesus.

Rachel (Rahel) is Hebrew and means "ewe." Rachel was Jacob's wife. The twelve tribes of Israel are all the descendants of "Jacob," whose name later became "Israel." The story is that Jacob worked for Rachel's father for seven years in order to earn her hand in marriage. Rachel's father tricked Jacob to work for another seven before allowing the marriage. Rachel was a popular Colonial American name for a girl and continues to be popular today.

Jonathan pronounced "Yawn-a-tahn" in Hebrew, means "the Lord has given." There are many historical Jonathans portrayed in the Bible but probably the one most remembered is Jonathan, the eldest son of King Saul the first king of Israel. Jonathan is also remembered by his close friendship with Biblical David. The name Jonathan is one of the most popular names in the western world. It has made its way into surnames in the form of Johnson and it's many versions. Millions of people have a Jonathan in their family tree. This does not mean the family was Jewish. One might though, take a look at the other names in the tree and see if they too have Hebrew origins.

Kenath means "possession." Mentioned in the Old Testament in the Book of Numbers, it was a town in an area of rich grazing lands, east of the Jordan river. The town of Kenath was taken by a Manasseh man named "Nobah." Nobah changed the name of Kenath to... Nobah. Kenath is an ancient city where I believe today you may find ruins.

The name **Jared** (or Jered) is seen in the history of the ancestry of Jesus. Jared was Enoch's father. Jared was a Judahite which meant he was an inhabitant of Judah or a member of the tribe of Judah. The name Jared means descent.

Joanna was a steward for King Herod and is known in the Biblical story as administering to Jesus. Joanna was among the group of women who went with Mary Magdalene to visit the tomb of Jesus. In the Biblical history of Mary and Joseph, the name is also seen as Joanan. Joanan was Joseph's ancestor, her name means "The lord has been gracious."

Hezekiah, also seen as Hizkiah, Hizkijah and Ezekias. He was the 12th king of Judah, considered one of the best. The name means Jehovah strengthens. Hezekiah was one of Jesus's ancestors and he had a very close relationship with Isaiah the prophet. Hezekiah is famous for not being fond of the worship of idols.

Many people believe that **Isaiah** was the greatest prophet of Biblical history. Also seen as Esaias, the name means "salvation of the Lord." Isaiah's prophecies will be forever tied to Jerusalem. He foresaw the destruction of Jerusalem and Judah but believed that a righteous remnant would persevere. Jesus is recorded (book of Luke) reading Isaiah (Esaias) writings. Perhaps the continuous Christian presence in Jerusalem is due in part, to Isaiah's promise to Gentiles, that they will participate in the spiritual inheritance of Israel.

There are quite a few **Michael**s mentioned in the Bible but one of the most important was Michael the special guardian of the Hebrews. He was considered an Archangel, which means he was an angel of high rank. Michael argued with Satan over Moses's body and Michael also fought a dragon in heaven. The name may mean "who is like God." There are other Biblical Michaels besides Michael the Archangel.

What an interesting guy **Noah** was. Who hasn't heard of Noah's Ark and who doesn't wonder how one guy could fit all the earth's species onto one boat? Noah was 10th down from Adam, the guy who made his famous entrance with Eve. But Noah was literally a cultured guy. In Genesis, he appears to culture vineyards and discovered the art of making wine. Noah's drunkenness creates quite a stir; you can find that story in the Bible too. Noah had a son named Shem and this is where the word "Semite" originated. Today we think of Semites as Jews and Arabs but this was not always the case. There were other Semite groups, including the Babylonians, Aramaeans, Phoenicians and Assyrians.

The original meaning of **Andrew** means "manliness." As a disciple of John the Baptist, Andrew was one of the twelve apostles (twelve men selected by Jesus to be with him). Like Jesus, Andrew was a fisherman. Andrew went to Greece to preach Jesus's teachings and it was in Greece where Andrew was crucified.

Isaac is a Hebrew name that originally meant "laughter." Isaac holds a special place in Jewish history, as it is from him that in the Book of Genesis, the "Chosen People" descend. His father and mother were Abraham and Sarah, his wife was Rebecca and his son was Jacob. So, in Jewish history, Isaac was a big deal and so were his family.

Aaron is an ancient Hebrew name. He was a Levite, which meant he was a member of the tribe of **Levi**. Who were the Levites? They assisted the tabernacle priests with the sacred vessels. The third book of the Jewish Law of Moses is Leviticus, which contains the ceremonial laws for the Levites and the priests. Leviticus is one of the books of the Bible. Aaron was the high priest of the Jews. He referred to the ceremonial laws of Leviticus for his divine instruction.

Chapter Three
Jewish Conquistadors

History of San Francisco mural "Conquistadors Discover the Pacific" by Anton Refregier at Rincon Annex Post Office located near the Embarcadero at 101 Spear Street, San Francisco, California

During the medieval era, crusading knights thought that they were the most civilized and advanced in all the world. Little did they know that the Turks saw them as ignorant barbarians. Because the Mohammedan culture was so much more advanced than that of the European crusaders, it caught the knights by surprise. Eastern civilization, with its art and culture, dazzled the knights. After the crusaders brought back precious stones, colorful rugs, spices and jewelry, the European people wanted more. Retrieving these fabulous treasures required the building of more ships and more bankers to handle the transactions. They needed more middlemen to sell the wares. Trading increased and brought great prosperity to European cities.

Allah is the name Mohammedans gave to their Supreme Being. Arabic-speaking Christians and Jews also use the expression *Allah*. It's a contraction, *Al-ilah*, meaning "the God." In Spain, during the $8^{th} - 11^{th}$ centuries, there existed what's known to Spanish Jewry as the *Golden Age*, where Jews and Muslims, under amicable Mohammedan rule, grew intellectually and culturally. In the years prior to 1492 (before Jews were completely expelled from Spain) they lived side by side with Muslims and other Spaniards. Many of the Jewish genealogical records from that era show Jews with Spanish surnames. It can be a surprise to find that a Spanish ancestor was a Muslim or a Jew and not a Christian.

The Moors from North Africa conquered Spain and Portugal (called the Iberian Peninsula in the early 700's) and gave refuge to the Sephardic Jews. Together they created and advanced Spain's Golden Age, particularly in Seville, Cordova and Toledo. Philosophy, medicine, mathematics, law and theology were discussed and studied by brilliant minds. By 1492, the Inquisition had devastated both the Moorish and Sephardic Jewish populations of Spain.

A good example of this side by side existence is the relationship between *The Great Rabbi* and the *Chivalrous*

Saladin. Known as Maimonides, this "great" Jewish rabbi, was exceptionally talented and brilliant in the fields of philosophy, math and astronomy. He was also an accomplished physician. Born in 1135, Maimonides (Mosheh ben Maimon) was the personal physician for the chivalrous Saracen leader, Saladin. Only two years older than Maimonides, Saladin was the son of a Kurdish military man who was the Governor of Damascus. Saladin fought for control of Egypt, against the Christians who allied with Egypt. Saladin eventually became the Sultan of both Egypt and Syria (1174-1193). He fiercely fought against the Crusades and is remembered by his ties to his opponent, Richard the Lion Hearted. Saladin conquered Jerusalem in 1187 from the Christian Crusaders. History remembers Saladin as having many admirable qualities; honor, devotion, kindness and a reputation as "the ideal knight."

In the late 1400's, Spain and Portugal enacted Inquisitions. Eventually, the Spanish Inquisition came to the New World. It extended into Mexico and became the Mexican Inquisition, bringing with it, the continued persecution of the Jews. One was arrested if they lacked the necessary certificate, *Pureza de la sangre*, which translated means, "purity of the blood," proving that one was **not** Jewish. The

Law of the Pure Blood was a prohibition against migrating to Mexico unless one could prove that the last three generations of their family had been "Old Christians." This law was enacted as an attempt to keep out Jews who'd fled Spain and Portugal's Inquisitions and were seeking a new homeland. With the threat of arrest, it's no wonder that many Sephardic Jews in the New World hid their ethnic roots. The abundance of Old Testament names in the Latin community today, are remnants of a religion and culture, much loved by those who were forced to abandon it. And as I wrote about in *Secret Genealogy*, countless Latinos living in America's southwest are finding that their ancestors were in fact Jewish but hid it, making them *Crypto-Jews*.

Imagine being arrested for not going to church. In 1480, when the Inquisition was only twelve years away, the Spanish crown decreed that heretics had about thirty days to confess their sins and convert to Christianity. Being a heretic meant big trouble. Part of a new law called the "Edict of Grace," encouraged friends and family to report those who refused to go with the program. If someone gave your name, you were arrested and expected to confess. As you can imagine, a medieval prison is not a pretty place, so wanting to return to their homes and families, people confessed to being heretics. It's ghastly to think that our ancestors may have become Christians because they were tortured into it, but alas, this is one of history's unpleasant truths.

First, We'll Set Up the Holy Brotherhood... Then We'll Persecute Everyone Who's Not Christian

Ever wonder how the Spanish Inquisition came to be? King Ferdinand married his cousin Isabella and the two of them went about reuniting their kingdom. Problem is... they had a cruel way of going about it. I guess they thought things would be better if everyone in the kingdom was one religion. They eventually succeeded, but at great cost to non-Christians.

Spain had a large Muslim population because for centuries, the country had been ruled by the Moors. Under Muslim rule, there were plenty of Jews because the Moors let them be. But the Christians finally won back the Spanish provinces and the king and queen were dead set on straightening things out... they wanted unity. There were also too many different languages and too much lawlessness. Some districts were ruled by religious leaders, while other regions had developed governments. Ancient Spain was in disarray.

So they brought out the mounted police, the *Holy Brotherhood* (Santa Hermandad), a police force on horseback who let feudal war lords know who was boss. Then the monarch set up their famous system of inquiry, *The Inquisition* it was called. They brought people into court for interrogation. Basically, it was… you're going to be a Christian. You are **not** going to *pretend* you are a Christian; you are really going to **be** a Christian. And if you're not, you'll be expelled from the kingdom. And by the way, on your way out… leave everything here, including your gold. Wealthy Moors and Jews, leave your land to the kingdom, your cattle also stays. And all those agricultural fields and trees you planted? We'll take that too!

What *really* made the monarch angry were the Moors and Jews who converted to Catholicism but who weren't *really* Christian. They hated that. Imagine the nerve of them, going to church on Sunday but when at home practicing Islam or Judaism. And Christians who didn't accept the monarch's idea of what it meant to be a Catholic… they were punished too. Ferdinand and Isabella burned people to death. They tied them to crosses and started fires at their feet. That's one of the reasons why the New World became populated. People were running from serious oppression but the Inquisition followed them. The *Mexican Inquisition* is an important part of many a family genealogy. Latin Catholics who take DNA tests are often surprised to find out that they have Jewish heritage. Well what do you know? Nobody said anything. Would you?

It was in 1501 when all Mohammedans who would not convert to Christianity, were purged from Spain. It was in 1492 when the Jews were purged. Some of the Moors and Jews banished from Spain wound up in America. Some of the expelled Moors and Jews went to Turkey, North Africa and Greece. You may have to listen hard for it, but in these regions, coming from the mouths of their descendants, you may find a corrupted form of their ancient Spanish language. King Ferdinand and Queen Isabella may have exiled them hundreds of years ago, but they could not exile the language.

A huge swath of America was at one time "New Spain." There is an ever-growing group of Catholics who have uncovered their Jewish heritage. In America, in almost every state, the most commonly spoken language other than

English, is Spanish. Maybe it is to the strong Crypto-Jewish movement in America's Southwest and Latin America that we can look for help in unraveling whether Crypto-Jews were a part of the Spanish Conquistador's invasion and destruction of the ancient empires of Mexico, Central and South America and the building of a vast network of Christian missions that spread into North America, furthering the spread of Christianity throughout the world. As ironic as it may sound.

Until I became a genealogist and learned that there is always more to the story, I never thought of Cortez or Pizarro as Jews. They were Spanish Conquistadors. Why should I think that they were Jews? Curiously, I looked up their surnames on the list of Sephardic Jews who were paid to leave Amsterdam between 1757 and 1813. That list was prepared a great many years after the Cortez/Pizarro era but still… there were four "Cortisos" and three "Pesaro." Here are six more historically significant names of the Conquistadors' secretaries and a soldier: de Estete, de Xerez, de la Hoz, de Mena, Ruiz de Arce and de Leon.

The names Mena, Ruiz, Arce, Leon and Hoz are on another list of expelled Jews, during the Spanish Inquisition.

Because their surname is on a list of Inquisitional Jews, does not prove that these men were Jewish but **no one** should think you a fool for desiring to research further.

The Spanish Conquistadors and the male "secretaries" who travelled with them, is a violent yet fascinating historical account. Mexico and Central and South America are also known as *Latin America*. Could some of the Conquistadors or the men who were part of the Spanish invasion of Latin America been Jews? And the secretaries (men enlisted by the Crown to keep a certified record of events) who travelled with the Conquistadors. Could they have been Jews?

Although these men were the invaders, they chronicled the beauty of the fortresses of the ancient Inca empire. They spoke of the Inca's "grand architecture" and their "sun temples." For tens of thousands of miles, this empire impressed the Spaniards with their "great" roads that ran through "deep valleys, high mountains, banks of snow, torrents of water, living rock, and wild rivers." They wrote that it was "clean" and "swept free of refuge."

The Incas had an oral history that spoke of white bearded strangers from the sea who would one day return. Does this tell us that the invading Spaniard's were fair-skinned? Who were the original "white bearded strangers from the sea?" Were they Vikings who had swiftly slashed their way through Europe and the Middle East? Whoever they were, they left an impression. The Incan rulers, in their curiosity, instead of defeating the invading Spaniards, let them reach their royal domains. By then it was too late. The Incan empire collapsed and the Spanish Conquistadors replaced it with Christianity. Years later, when much of the history was recorded, it was viewed through the eyes of Christians. That must be taken into account. But so must the idea that some of the invaders may have been Jews.

Chapter Four

Origins

Abbey of Kells - Scanned from Treasures of Irish Art, 1500 B.C. to 1500 a.D. : From the Collections of the National Museum of Ireland, Royal Irish Academy, & Trinity College, Dublin, Metropolitan Museum of Art & Alfred A. Knopf, New York, 1977, ISBN 0394428072

At the close of the American Revolution, when the Constitution was written, there was jealousy between different sectors. Southern states were farming states, New England states were trading states. Therefore, manufacturing became important to New England. The farming states wanted good prices on commodities. New England states wanted laws enacted that taxed foreign ships, so that they might get all of the shipping business.

Some of the northern states wanted to give Congress the power to forbid the importation of African slaves. Some of the southern states would not consent to such a plan. So it had been agreed that Congress might pass navigation laws. And might forbid the slave trade after twenty years. There were other disputes about whether slaves should be counted in regard to taxes and in deciding the **number of congressional representatives a state should have**. These disputes had been settled by counting five blacks as equal to three whites. The blacks did not vote, so white slave owners had more influence than non-slave owning northerners.

The settlers of the New England states (Northerners) came for the most part, from English **towns**. Once here, they settled in little towns. A large part of the settlers of Maryland, Virginia and the Carolinas (Southerners) came from the English **countryside**. Their dreams were to build large rural estates (think plantations). After the English King Charles I, was put to death, many of his aristocratic followers went to Virginia. While some members of the English aristocracy settled in the North and many men of Puritan ideas came to the South, a historian may well say that New England was Puritan and that the South was aristocratic in some sections, though not in all.

Keeping track of the demographics of regions will never be an exact science. Imagine today, being at an event of 50,000 people and trying to record where they all came from. It's just not possible. Yet, we love to try and do that with history and we weren't even there. But thank goodness for scholars who try. We love them for that. They've done a good job. The evidence of their hard work is everywhere. It turns up prominently in genealogy.

In 1630, William Bradford, the second governor of the colony of Massachusetts, began compiling his notes. His *History of Plymouth Plantation* is considered the most important reading of the Pilgrims and their colony. I found it on the Internet and have tried to read it. Some of the letters are missing from the words. I suppose the ink did not stick well and it was kept in its original version. I question whether I will ever make it through the whole journal and I admit to doing a lot of scanning. But if you love history, and especially if you have New England ancestry, it's an interesting peek into the past. I found several things that interested me. One is that the *Walloons* inhabited southern Massachusetts and were termed *Gallois*. Let's explore that.

Walloon is a French word *Walon*, designating people, primarily of Celtic origin, inhabiting southern Belgium. Walloon also designates the language of these Celtic people, the *Belgian French*.

Gallois stems from *Gallus*. It's Latin and it means *Gaul*, or *Gallic*. My old dictionary says that *Gallo* denotes French.

William Bradford is telling us that the earliest inhabitants of southern Massachusetts were French, of Celtic origin. Immigrants from southern Belgium. When he said that the term for these people was Gallois, today one might say that they were French. But it is not that simple. Their history moves through several different lands. I've read about ancient Celtic ruins in the hills above the southern Mediterranean. And when we think of Celts, many picture those with red hair but I've seen online discussions where the stereotypes that are represented at Celtic festivals are laughed at. I've read of Egyptian pharaohs with red hair. They were not "Celts." Or were they? The history of the Celts is confusing. No doubt, who the Celts are today is vastly different from who they were originally. Their historical roots go back to the Middle East. DNA studies have confirmed that the ancestors of the Irish came from the Biblical lands.

Some of the more recent ancestors of the Irish are those from Northern Spain. But Stone Age ancestors (with a tendency toward black hair and brown eyes) who came from the Holy Land, also contributed to the genetic make-up of the Irish. Researchers say that the Irish and the Scots are genetically similar. When the Irish invaded the Scots, they brought tall genes, low body fat, athletic build, fair-skin and red hair. If you're confused maybe this will help. The ancient Irish text, *Leabhar Gabhla* (the Book of Invasions) tells of Ireland's earliest settlers who came in waves. The first were the small dark people, *Fir Bolg*. The next were the *Tuatha de Danaan*, a magical super-race. And lastly, the *Milesians*, the sons of Mil, the soldier from Spain. The Milesians became the rulers.

Here is a chart I made of Irish names. It might help to pinpoint the region of your Irish ancestors:
"O" means "of"
"Mac" means son of
O'Connor is common in the west- Connaught Ireland
Ma'c Carthy is common in the south- Munster Ireland

O'Neill, O'Donnell is common in the north- Ulster Ireland

MacLochlann is common in the north- Ulster Ireland

O'Byrne & O'Toole is common in the east Leinster Ireland

(You may try putting Mac, Mc or O' in front of the surname you're searching, as it may have been spelled that way before.)

In America's Midwest, you'll find pockets of Polish settlements. When driving through Indiana, I noticed small towns that were settled by Polish pioneers. I have an acquaintance who comes from one of those small, Polish, Indiana towns and she married a Jewish man. She's quite proud of her ancestry and does not seem to relate or have any knowledge of Jewish ancestry but she laughs when she recalls her husband telling her, "When I first met you, I thought you were a nice little Jewish girl." My hunch is that some of America's Midwesterners with ancestors from Poland or Eastern Europe, may have Jewish ancestry. A study of that would be interesting.

When Jews were mistreated and expelled from European lands, they longed for peace and security. During the middle ages, Europe was home to many religions but Medieval rulers were not always tolerant of faiths other than their own. Catholics, Protestants, Muslims, Jews and Pagans called Europe home but they weren't always welcome. However, in the middle 1300's, Polish King, Casimir the Great welcomed the Jews. They came to his country from Italy, Spain, France, England, Germany and Bohemia. Perhaps they are the ancestors of some of America's Midwestern Polish populations. No doubt when the Nazis rounded up Poland's Jews and escorted them to their deaths, many were the descendants of Jews who had many years before, accepted the welcome hospitality of King Casimir.

In 1648, massacres in Poland drove the Jews to Amsterdam. When they arrived, the Jews already living there were the Sephardim. They looked down their noses at the Polish

Ashkenazic Jews. And denied them burials in their cemeteries. The Ashkenazi were poor but they were industrious. Many were skilled jewelers and knew the art of diamond polishing. Through the years, they gained a foothold in the Netherlands (and Belgium) and those who immigrated to other Western European countries and America, have left their mark. Their descendants are often wealthy diamond merchants or probably in some cases, Indiana farmers who haven't a clue that their ancestors were Jews.

Americans with English ancestry might research their roots better by understanding that the Jews in England during the 1600's were mainly the Sephardim but as the century moved forward, the Ashkenazi became stronger in population.

Every time I see a city or a town with Biblical name, it gives me a start. Egyptian and Greek names do as well. My mind says, *what's up with that?* I googled "cities and towns that have Hebrew names." Up came an article from twenty-one-years ago.

A Jewish women's organization called *Hadassah*, was curious about the same thing. They began an investigation as to why the early American founders chose Biblical names for their cities and towns. Names like Bethlehem, Hebron, Canaan, Zion, Jordan, Jericho, Pisgah, Mitzpah and Gilead fascinated the Hadassah. Especially intriguing was that more than half the states in America have a city or town named either *Jerusalem* or *Salem*. They believed that researching the reasons for the Hebrew names would reveal *how Jews have been treated in America.*

The organization's director for Hebrew Education, Carol Diament, wrote that *there is no doubt those who founded this country likened it to Zion and themselves to the Children of Israel*. But Moshe Davis of the Hebrew University of Jerusalem, believed that America's founding fathers substituted Egypt for Britain and related to the Jews when they were held as slaves. In his understanding, the founding fathers related to Jewish suffering and therefore *welcomed the Jews to America*. It fit in with America's ideas of *civil liberty*.

Historian Rabbi Arthur Hertzberg had a different opinion. He believed that "The Puritans of New England were obsessed by the Jewish Bible, but they were not hospitable to the Jews or Judaism." It does seem that there is and has been throughout America's history, an obsession with the "Jewish Bible." And judging by the Hebrew names of the cities, the Holy Land as well.

Let me share what I've deciphered about some of the geography of the Holy Land. It's difficult when an area is known by many names. The Holy Land, Palestine, Canaan, Israel, Phoenicia, Judah. It's a lot like the changing names and boundaries of Russia, USSR, Ukraine, Soviet Union, etc. Wars commence, territories vary and boundaries change.

Canaan was Noah's grandson and the patriarch of the Canaanites. (Noah cursed his grandson Canaan but that's another story). The Canaanites of the north separated themselves from the Canaanites of Israel and became the powerful nation of Phoenicia. They worshiped what Moses called idols, including a sun god they called Baal and a moon goddess they called Ashtoreth or Astarte. They had depraved religious ceremonies that included sacrificing children. What's known as Canaan was Western Palestine, a geographical area surrounded by the Dead Sea, the Mediterranean Sea and the Sea of Galilee. Moses instructed the Israelites to remove all the Canaanites (Phoenicians) from Palestine (Canaan) because they worshiped idols and he feared they would lead the Israelites astray. The Ancient Israelites had a prophecy that Canaan was the land of milk and honey and that God promised it to them for "life everlasting."

Chapter Five
A Bit About the Brits

When genetic researchers speak of the *British* people, they also mean those of Scotland, Ireland and Wales. In their studies, they found only a miniscule amount of Roman DNA among the modern British. The reason for this is because during the first two-hundred years of the Roman occupation of Britain (43 A.D. – 410) their rulers forbade their subjects to marry the native people. So the Brits are not as Roman as some might assume. Nor are the English Brits as Germanic as they may have assumed.

During the Victorian era, England had a passion for Germany. Many English Brits saw it as their heritage and even spoke German and enjoyed the music and classic literature. They loved to vacation in Germany. But when World War II broke out and the Third Reich came into power, the English obsession with German culture dropped substantially. Nonetheless, science is uncovering that the English are not near as Germanic as they had originally thought. Most descend from ancient people who were indigenous to the area before the Celts, or the Romans or the

Normans arrived. (See *Secret Genealogy III - From Jewish-Anglo-Saxon Tribes to New France Acadians.*)

But the Anglo-Saxon tribes did play a role in English history, especially with the British Royal family. The British Royal Family was at one time known as the *House of Saxe-Coburg and Gotha.* Because it sounded too Germanic, during World War I, so King George V changed it to the *Royal House of Windsor.* Since 1917, the British Royal Family has used the House of Windsor title. The name derives from Windsor Castle in Berkshire, England. The Royal Family descends from William the Conqueror and it was during his era that the use of a coat of arms began. Although William was of Viking descent (a man from the north, a Norman, Scandinavian) he had settled in northern France (Normandy) so you'll see a lot of French words in coats of arms and in English mottos. In the early years of English history, the rulers spoke French. It was the peasants who spoke English.

The coat of arms, also known as *heraldry* refers to the symbol a chieftain or lord used to identify his fiefdom. This symbol was displayed in a banner, on his coat, on his soldier's coats and on their armament. This is where the expression "coat of arms" originated. During this medieval era, they called a messenger a "herald." Because messengers wore their lord's symbol on their coats and probably on their horse's saddle and maybe carried a small banner with their insignia, the castle guards would look down and recognize the herald's symbol. When there was a marriage between families, each having their own coat of arms, they were combined.

This is the flag of the Federal Republic of Germany

Quote

Saxons. Teutonic people, whose territory has greatly varied in historic times. Their name probably signifies swordsmen. Ptolemy (c. A.D. 150) states that they inhabited Slesvig and three islands off its W. coast. In 286 they appear as pirates in the North Sea and English Channel, and by about 350 they had crossed the Elbe and extended their sway almost to the Rhine. In the 5th century they had made settlements at

Bayeux and the mouth of the Loire, and according to Bede were associated with the Angles and Jutes in the conquest of Britain. The names Esses, Middlesex, Sussex, and Wessex, which contain their name, support the theory that their settlements were confined to S. England, but it is very doubtful whether any distinction can be made between the Saxon and Anglian settlers, as they all called themselves Angles, and were all called Saxons by foreigners, as is still done by the Welsh and Highlanders. Grolier Encyclopedia, Vol. 17 & 18, pg 246.

Chapter Six

The Renaissance

The Last Supper, Leonardo da Vinci

Scholars concluded years ago that brute force played a role in shaping ancient tribes. But most of the power lay in the hands of the magician. Because superstition is so powerful, the charismatic personality who "appears" to be controlling the growth of crops, driving away plagues and controlling the rain, gains the edge in this battle between brains and brawn.

Primitive society's "elite" were charismatic elders who convinced others that they held the magical power. Tribal members believed that the "magician" could bring better life for all. When primitive people believed that the elder magician had this power over them, the superstition was more powerful than the threat of physical violence. Therefore, the magicians out-smarted the warriors in the fight for power. The Ancients found it was more powerful to *control people's minds* through fear of what *could* happen. Young warriors who thought of challenging elder leaders, would back down out of fear. They feared that a spell would be cast upon them. That fear carries a strong psychological impact. It overwhelms people into thinking that they are sick. Even today, people are known to die because they believe it so strongly.

Convincing the rest of the group that you have supernatural powers will make you a God or Goddess. That was the way it was for ancient tribes and no doubt, today, that kind of thinking works in business and politics. If the "power" was believed to be passed to the wizard's son or relative, the position was handed down. The heir to the throne, so to speak. We see this in modern political families. The great talker, the great negotiator, convinces us that their heir is the next great political wizard. If a man had magical powers *and* the skill of a warrior, he became king and his son or nephew inherited the title whether they were competent or not.

Eventually, magicians and wizards found their way into secret societies. As discussed in *Secret Genealogy III*, one of the earliest secret societies began with cryptic meetings of the disciples of *Pythagoras,* a Greek mathematician who lived 500 or more years before Jesus. As a young man, Pythagoras traveled to Egypt and Lebanon where he was initiated into the Phoenicians' *Ancient Mysteries*. After the destruction of the first temple in Jerusalem, Pythagoras spent time at a temple in Haifa, Israel before returning to Egypt where the "Ancient Mysteries" originated. In Egypt, Pythagoras studied the mysteries for about two decades. He is also believed to have studied in Babylon for over a decade.

Pythagoras's followers didn't trim their fingernails, didn't shave and did not cut their hair, so they probably had long dreadlocks. It was quite pagan and very esoteric. People from both the upper and lower classes respected his wisdom. The *Pythagorean Brotherhood* designed the multiplication table, enabling ancient engineers to answer the era's pressing questions. Centuries later, the Pythagorean multiplication table continued to provide answers in the building trades, astronomy and all the multitude ways mathematics help us build, explore and count. Because geometry was so important to the Pythagoreans, some of their tombs have the quadrant, level, cubit or square etched into their tombs.

The Pythagorean school that the famous mathematical wizard created in Southern Italy over 2,000 years ago, was an illegal destination for women. Because the group was secretive, and the brotherhood tight-lipped, only the bravest of women attended their meetings. Some of the more famous historical names of Pythagorean followers were Plato, Aristotle, Hippocrates and Socrates. Plato is attributed to dispersing theories of the brotherhood throughout Italy and into Egypt, where Pythagoras had originally studied and was initiated into the mysteries. What role Pythagorean's female followers played is unclear but women's role in the spread of Christianity is huge, its growth in ancient Italy is attributed to women convincing the men in their lives to accept the new religion. So women may have played a substantial role.

A lot of the philosophy of the Pythagorean brotherhood was taken from the *Old Testament* and *Judaism*. Besides advancing the study of mathematics, the tightly knit community of Pythagoreans studied the natural sciences and had philosophical discussions. Two thousand years later, during the 1500's, men of "science" continued to meet in secret. During that era, the *Invisible College* sprang up. And from the seeds of the *Invisible College*, grew Britain's *Royal Society*.

The Pythagoreans loved the five-pointed star, known as *Solomon's Seal*, referring to King Solomon, king of the two kingdoms, Israel and Judah. The ancient Pythagorean Brotherhood believed that the five-pointed star symbolized health and well-being. This *pentagram* was the secret recognition sign between the brotherhood. Interesting that the *Solomon's Seal*, now seen upon the flag of Israel, was also associated with guarding against disease. Sounds like the same star, although it is six-pointed, many believe the five-pointed star was what it was originally. It is also known as the *Star of David* or the *Shield of David*. Makes sense. Solomon's father was, after all, King David. Today, the iconic symbol of the *Freemasons* is the six-pointed star, leading one to suspect that the secret brotherhood proudly traces its origins back to the ancient Pythagoreans and the ancient Pythagoreans to ancient Judaism. At least an *association*.

The Pythagoreans guarded their secrets well; their meetings were cryptic and those who belonged were forbidden to speak of their discoveries. But this secrecy came with a price. The ancient Italian government, in power at that time, grew suspicious and forced the closure of the mathematical wizard's school. Eventually Pythagoras was murdered by those who opposed his teachings. Secrecy, and the fear it conjured in the general population, brought the demise of the Pythagorean Brotherhood.

During the Middle Ages, many leaders viewed science as mystic and filled with witchcraft, so they stopped progress every chance they got. Brilliant minds were squelched and visionaries were imprisoned. It was dangerous to be a free-thinker. Some of these intellectuals were labeled as *illuminato*, an Italian word for those who claim spiritual or intellectual illumination. When these illuminato were members of special sects or groups, the word was capitalized, the *Illuminati*. In Latin, the word is *illuminatus*. In Italian, it is *illuminato* and it refers to those who claim special illumination.

Pagan Europe was not without culture. They had poetry, sculpture, plays, pottery, ornamentation and architecture. But after Europe adopted Christianity, the pagan culture was not viewed favorably. Early European Christianity brought the belief that it was desirable to free oneself of worldly pleasures and seek enlightenment through service to others. America's Puritan past is a good example of this. But the Renaissance was a revival of the art and culture of the ancient pagan pleasure seekers. And for many, a rebellion against the restrictions of Christianity.

When people speak of art, antiques or other cultural objects, they'll often use the expression, "Renaissance Period." Taken from the French word *renaitre*, which means *to be born again*. The Renaissance era was a time when people developed an appreciation for ancient culture, particularly that of Rome and Greece. Although the forerunner of the Renaissance movement was a man named Francesco Petrarca, who lived from 1304-74, the time period for the Renaissance was the 14th - 16th centuries, or 1500's - 1700's.

During the Renaissance period, a 15th century English sect (inspired by the second chapter of Daniel, the interpretation of Daniel's dream) believed that the Messiah was soon to return and that he would reign as king for a thousand years. Known as *Fifth Monarchy Men*, members of this fanatical sect believed that they must use force to establish the coming Christian monarchy. There were many messianic sects that sprang up around this time, including Jewish fanatics who gave up everything they owned in Europe to travel to Jerusalem to meet their messiah and the new era. The reason for the growth of these fanatic sects was the coming date...

1666. The Old Testament was inspiration for the *fifth monarchy*. The Old Testament was originally known as the *Old Covenant*. The covenant existed as a treaty between God and the children of Israel.

Many of us grew up thinking that the Bible was one big book. The original Greek word for Bible meant "books." Not "book." When were they written? Over a period of about 1,600 years. The first part of the Bible is the Old Testament written before the life of Jesus. It contains thirty-nine books. After the influence of the life of Jesus, the Christians created a new "treaty," the *New Testament*. It focused on Jesus as the Messiah, it has twenty-seven books. Thirty-nine Old Testament and twenty-seven New Testament. That's sixty-six books.

Matthew, the fellow who wrote the Gospel, one of four "Gospels" in the Bible, was also a Jewish tax collector. Matthew believed that Jesus was the Messiah and legend has it that he was "called" by Jesus. Scholars take writings and analyze them and discover that books of the Bible were not written by one author but by several, Matthew is one of those authors. But what I find interesting is that Mathew's Gospel was directed not at Christians but at Jews, because Matthew was a Jew trying to convince other Jews that Jesus was the messiah. The Roman Catholic Church as well as Greek Churches and the Anglican Church accept Matthew as a *Saint*.

It's interesting to think that during times of antiquity when it was fashionable to worship "multiple" gods, that it would be heresy to believe in the concept of "one" god. When studying the ancient mysteries, we are led to the Jews, monotheism and early Freemasons who met in secret to share these mysteries.

Chapter Seven

Secret Societies ... Freemasons, Odd Fellows

California's gold country is a wonderful specimen of early American life, culture and society. People from all persuasions immigrated to California hoping to get rich. Although the West was not as conservative as other regions of the country, and predominantly male, as the 1800's progressed, women and families arrived in the gold mining towns. Looking at gold country history, we see a microcosm of American life. And perhaps the world, because of the immigrants who arrived from Europe, the Middle East and Asia to partake in the industry. The era leaves us endless books and newspapers that we can study.

The gold country has a long history of secret societies. The old buildings still stand and the organizations remain intact. A look at some of the tombstones tell us the old-timers were members of fraternal organizations. What were they? Benevolent societies? Trade guilds? Better Business

Bureaus or Chambers of Commerce? Did they emerge to serve the needs of the new territory in the same way that communities use local churches as community centers? In Sonora, California, another gold rush town, the Jewish community donated the Odd Fellows building to the town. In return, they asked that it be made available to them to use during *Jewish High Holiday* services.

Quote
"From the later obituary in the Hebrew we discover that Hannah Gumpert was 'for many years afflicted with an incurable nervous disorder,' that she was the mother of three 'interesting' children, and that the Odd Fellows and their wives came to her funeral in great numbers."
Pg 24, A Traveler's Guide to Pioneer Jewish Cemeteries of the California Gold Rush, by Susan Morris.

Jewish inclusion in 1800's California gold country Freemasonry, was common. In one instance, when a Jewish member died, the marching band for his funeral procession was ordered by the Freemasons. The funeral procession was five-hundred people strong. That's a huge funeral, even by today's standards. Other Jewish gold country businessmen were members of the Masons, evident by the carved symbols on their gravestones. Some were members of both the Freemasons *and* the Odd Fellows.

Quote

"Jews lived in multiethnic, multilingual, communities whose residents came from areas as diverse as New England, the American South and Midwest, Italy, Germany, Ireland, France, and China. Of necessity, these Gold Rush towns developed new patterns of integration, and Jews were an integral part of the new communities, joining the Masons, Odd Fellows, fire brigades, political parties, and cultural and charitable organizations."

Pg 4, A Traveler's Guide to Pioneer Jewish Cemeteries of the California Gold Rush, by Susan Morris.

A Masonic Fraternity is a Freemason association of men who believe in a supreme being and hold common interests in business. The Freemason brotherhood usually holds men of similar character and social status. Masonic Fraternities of men hold regular meetings and have for centuries. Initiation rites are performed, as are other rituals. The *brotherhood* is sworn to secrecy, leading outsiders to constantly speculate just what "mysteries" the Freemasons hold.

Masonic rituals vary within regions. One area may use Islamic icons for their rituals while another may use those based on Judaism and Christianity. If you see a five-pointed star on someone's garage or barn, one would probably have to ask individual barn owners what their star symbolized. Maybe in Kentucky we'd receive answers referring to the Civil War, while in Indiana it could indicate folk art. I pass one regularly out in front of a BBQ restaurant and I suspect it is meant to give one the impression of Texas. Stars are popular everywhere but depending upon how they are poised, sometimes you get the feeling it is a political or philosophical statement. They may be declaring that members of either the *Freemasons* or their female counterparts, the *Eastern Star*, reside there. Maybe, like the *Star of David* that adorns the flag of the nation of Israel, it is intended to protect the inhabitants' health and wellbeing.

The weirdest thing happened to me a few years ago. It was a dark, stormy night (seriously) and I thought I would get on the web and see if I could find secrets regarding my family's ties to Freemasonry. I googled Knights Templar and started pulling up some pretty trippy UK websites. I was using my father's name to see if I had ancestry by the same name. I found some interesting info so I clicked on "print." The printer made all kinds of noise and made marks on the paper but the only thing it printed was one word, "why?" As the thunder clapped outside and the wind and pounding rain shook the windowpane next to me, I was spellbound. It was probably just a strange co-incidence but I must say, it felt like someone was monitoring my research and wanted to know "why" I wanted to know about Celtic Freemasonry and my family name. A similar thing happened years later. I was attempting to publish the first *Secret Genealogy* (a how-to for finding Jewish genealogy) on an online German eBook site. When I looked at the results, there was nothing but gobbly goop. Nothing decipherable except these words, "stay alive." This time I shuddered. Was I being threatened? I tried several more times to upload the book. Eventually I succeeded and I had no further problems.

When I saw the names of the close associates of my mother's ancestors, I began to see a conspiracy. And when I paired it with the fact that both my mother and father's "people" were deeply embedded into Freemasonry, I began to believe that there must be a connection between the Masons and Crypto-Jews. *Was that what was so secret?* A haven from the outside world? A group sworn to secrecy where they could create their own style of worship and a bond so strong none would tell?

One day, I was making plum jam and I pulled out an old canning jar and on the front, was a big five-pointed star with the words: MASON JAR. All roads don't lead to Freemasonry but sometimes it seems that way. The design of the jar was originally patented by a man named John L. Mason, who was not a Freemason. His patent wasn't protected well enough so other manufacturers cashed in on it. The Ball brothers, who made the Mason jar famous, were Freemasons who belonged to the Scottish Rite.

When I'm doing genealogical research on the Internet, it doesn't take long before I'm led to one or the other Masonic connections. Take my husband's French Canadian ancestry as a perfect example. I am researching the surname, "Chartier." It goes back to the surname "Dit Benac." I google "Dit Benac" and I see a lot of options for genealogical webpages and I look forward to reading them. But out of habit I googled "Jewish Dit Benac" and sure enough, here come the ancient Freemasons.
This is the website:
http://www.phoenixmasonry.org/mackeys_encyclopedia/m.htm

ENCYCLOPEDIA OF FREEMASONRY AND ITS KINDRED SCIENCES
by ALBERT C. MACKEY M. D.

It's interesting to think that during times of antiquity it was fashionable to worship "multiple" gods and *heresy* to worship only "one" god. Like I said, when studying the ancient mysteries, we're led to the Jews, monotheism and early Freemasons. They met in secret to share these mysteries. Just as today's medical breakthroughs are top secret until a patent is obtained, so it was during the Middle Ages. It was considered *sacred knowledge* to know which powerful medicines were obtained from which natural sources. The history of the fight over seeds from the cinchona tree, the source of quinine, between several different countries and the eventual creation of a worldwide monopoly by the Dutch is a good example of early corporate espionage.

Back in the 1500's, the Dutch created the first stock "exchange." The VOC (Vereenigde Oostindische Compagnie) that was the "Dutch East India Company." Investors got together and commissioned ships to bring back spices, cloth, herring, wheat, etc. The VOC was where you went to purchase your "share" in it. If pirates didn't get your ship or storms didn't ruin your wheat, you made a profit. This built the great Golden era of Amsterdam. The *New York Stock Exchange* is the successor of the original Dutch medieval exchange.

In 1684, fifteen Jewish families immigrated to Rhode Island. Their "rights to settle" was confirmed by the General Assembly. They brought with them, the first degrees of masonry. In 1872 "thirteen" Freemasons met at New York's Masonic Hall on East "Thirteenth" Street to create a North American organization of the *Ancient Order of the Nobles of the Mystic Shrine*. (It was on the "thirteenth" day in 1307 when France's King Phillip ordered the Knights Templar rounded up and put into chains.)

A Templar is a knight of the *Order of the Temple*, (referring to Solomon's Temple that the knights protected in Jerusalem during the Crusades). The Knights Templar are Freemasons. What do they have to do with Colonial America? Why are the Knights Templar credited with establishing the first banking system? After the Inquisition did the Knights Templar pirate ships? Why the Star of David in the Masonic Lodge? And what's the story with the Freemason apron?

Sounds like a good name for a rock band, *The Freemason Apron*. While I was reading about the ancient Hittites and what they were up to several-thousand years ago, with their horned helmets and aprons (the horns representing their bull-cult) I couldn't help but be reminded of the Freemasons. With the Hittites, the more horns they had, the more seniority they possessed. The Hittites also carried horn-shaped weapons and their pointed shoes were meant to resemble bull's horns. The Hittite's male "gods" wore an apron too. This website, www.hillcrestlodge397.com, explains it thusly: "As a badge of honor, the Lambskin Apron spells out honesty of purpose, integrity, uprightness of character, and soundness of moral principle."

Here are a few Freemason branches:

The Scottish Rite is a branch of the Freemasons. An early Freemason lodge in Edinburgh Scotland has record books that date back to 1599, although their beginnings go further back.

The **Mystic Order of Veiled Prophets of the Enchanted Realm** is a "social body" requiring Masonic membership to join. Also called **"The Grotto,"** it began in New York in

1889. The Order consists of Master Masons who fraternize casually for fun and relaxation.

The Ancient Arabic Order of the Nobles of the Mystic Shrine is a "social body" requiring Masonic membership in order to join. Also known as **"The Shrine"** and **"Shriners."** Designed as a charitable fraternity of Freemasons, the Imperial Council of the Ancient *Egyptian* Arabic Order of the Nobles of the Mystic Shrine of North and South America, contains members from African Masonic Lodges, including the African Lodge #1 created on July 3, 1776 in Massachusetts. This Freemason organization believes in fostering educational, civic and economic opportunities across the globe and "maintains a dialogue with White House officials and Congress."

The **"Imperial Court Daughters of Isis"** are the wives, mothers, sisters and daughters of the Freemasons' social, charitable fraternity, the **"Ancient Egyptian Arabic Order of the Nobles of the Mystic Shrine."** The Freemason woman's auxiliary is over a hundred years old.

Whether the Freemasons are benevolent or not, depends on with whom you speak. After years of writing about the cryptic and often wicked intentions of secret societies, best-selling author Dan Brown, seems to think that today's Freemasons are benevolent. I saw him interviewed on T.V.

Some people wonder if Brown is Jewish. I don't think he is. The only thing I *can* tell you is that his name gives us two clues. His first name is Dan, no doubt from the Old Testament *Daniel* and the last name Brown brings me to something I wrote about *colors* in the first *Secret Genealogy* book:

If you were forced to convert to Christianity *and* forced to come up with a new name, what would you do? How could you rebel without being killed or exiled? Some Jews had no desire to take Christian names so they drew their names from nature by picking plants, bushes, trees or chose the names of places. Many surnames that are *colors* were chosen by Jews rather than picking Christian ones.

Dan Brown has brought the art of conspiracies to us in books and movies. Millions of people enjoy his work. He has his detractors though and I can imagine that he has received some angry letters. His writing is controversial. You know what they say, *never argue religion or politics.* I think it's fair to say he's guilty of breaking that cardinal rule. (Yes, pun intended.) His books and the movies produced from them are dramatic and fun. They entertain us and inform us about ancient history and remind us that mischief in the political and religious realms have been going on for thousands of years. And many a scholar is quick to remind us that the author did not always get his facts straight.

That said, there are plenty of deeply rooted conspiracy theories about secret societies. It's no secret that leaders throughout history have committed horrific crimes. Secret societies included. But I suspect that today, for the most part, men join the Freemasons to network within their communities, hoping it will help them prosper. In all realms; business, religion, politics, there are always exceptions. Those exceptions, coupled with ancient history's crudeness, give rise to all manner of theories. Books and movies like *The Da Vinci Code*, fan those flames.

Princess Diana's death is a perfect example. There are conspiracy theories put forth that her death was not an accident, but that a nefarious Freemasonry cult used her as a symbolic sacrifice. There's the belief that because she was associating with extremely powerful and wealthy Arabs (of whom the queen did not approve) she was assassinated. If you need more detail on these conspiracies, you'll have to google them. The story of Princess Diana's death is unfortunate. The world lost an admirable woman. She was named after an ancient goddess. There's even a conspiracy theory surrounding her name.

The Greeks had a mythological goddess named Artemis. The Romans called her Diana. (Diana means goddess.) She was the daughter of Zeus and the sister of Apollo. She's associated with hunting and you'll see her with a bow and arrow. Diana… nature goddess… virgin goddess. And for women who worshipped her during childbirth, she was the moon-goddess. Artemis is even mentioned in the Bible and through the ages, who and what Artemis (Diana) was, grew **distorted** from the original Greek myth, even evoking human sacrifice. Thus, the connection to the conspiracy that she was killed and that the tragic car accident in Paris was deliberate.

Famous people are always subject to scrutiny. During the 2016 presidential election, a man called into a San Francisco radio station talk show (KGO) and said that Donald Trump was a member of *the Knights of Malta*. It sounded like Freemasonry or an ancient fraternity left over from the Christian Crusades, so I looked into it.

Here is some interesting history about Malta and its knights, taken (and reworded) from the Grolier Encyclopedia: The Phoenicians colonized Malta about the 10th century B.C.E. and used it for trading. Then the Greeks in the 8th century B.C.E., then the Carthaginians in the 5th B.C.E. and then it fell to Rome in the 3rd B.C.E. The Vandals and Goths ravaged it in the 5th century A.D. but Belisarius drove them away and attached Malta to the Byzantine empire (Turks). The Moors (Muslims) seized it in the 9th century and pirated from the island. The Normans (think Vikings) ran the Moors off and after that Malta was a dependency of Sicily (think Italy). It was later given by marriage to the house of Hohenstaufen (medieval German rulers). Later the king of Argon (Spain) took charge and Charles V inherited it. It looks like Charles V gave Malta to the Knights of St. John in 1530 and it had a "glorious period." (The Knights of St. John had been driven from Rhodes by the Turks.)

Napoleon took Malta on his way to Egypt in 1798, the British blockaded and the French surrendered in 1800. The island was supposed to be restored to the Knights of St. John but the Maltese refused that promise and were granted the protection of Great Britain in 1814.

So who are the Knights of Malta? Are they the Knights of St. John who were refused by the Maltese or are they Knights of Maltese who refused the Knights of St. John? Another entry in the encyclopedia has this:

"Maltese Cross. Badge of the order of the Knights of Malta."

On one of the covers of *Newsweek*, Queen Elizabeth II's Jubilee was featured. Visible is what looks like a Maltese cross in her crown, bringing images of Hitler's Third Reich. But this cross was used long before Hitler used it. Besides representing Christianity, it may also symbolize heroism and impeccable leadership. The Maltese cross in her crown, serves as a reminder that even though England has become extremely multi-cultural, Germanic tribes played a role in its development.

Before 1917, the Royal Family used the title the *House of Saxe-Coburg and Gotha*. Saxe refers to the Saxones (as in Anglo-Saxon) and Gotha (Gothic) refers to the Teutonic tribes who encompass a broad range of people, especially Germanic. The *Saxe-Coburg and Gotha* title sounded too Germanic, so King George V changed it to the Royal House of Windsor during World War I.

Chapter Eight

The Bible, The Apostles & The Holy Family

Madonna with the book, Sandro Botticelli, 1483

The first four books of the New Testament (Matthew, Mark, Luke and John) tell the tale of the life of Jesus and his doctrines, and is known as *the Gospel*. That's what's referred to when we hear "preaching the Gospel." Gospel means *godspell* or *good tidings* and is based on the Anglo-Saxon word, spell, which means a saying, a tale or a speech, with elements of magical power and the ability to charm, or influence.

Jesus had twelve apostles and they were all Jewish. They are also known as the *disciples of Jesus*. The word apostle is from the Greek *apostolos*, meaning "one sent forth." These men were "sent forth to preach the gospel." The original twelve apostles included: Simon Peter, Andrew, James and John (sons of Zebedee), Philip, Bartholomew, Matthew (or Levi), Thomas (or Didymus), James (son of Alphaeus), Jude (or Thaddaeus), Simon the Cananaean, and Judas Iscariot. Matthias was chosen by lot to take the place of Judas. Paul, though not of the twelve, was equal to the others in office and dignity. And Barnabas, Paul's companion on his first missionary journey, is sometimes called an apostle.

The apostles religious beliefs are summarized in a **Catholic** version of the Apostles' Creed:

I believe in God, the Father almighty, creator of heaven and earth.
I believe in Jesus Christ, God's only Son, our Lord, who was conceived by the Holy Spirit, born of the Virgin Mary, suffered under Pontius Pilate, was crucified, died, and was buried; he descended into hell. On the third day he rose again; he ascended into heaven, he is seated at the right hand of the Father, and he will come to judge the living and the dead. I believe in the Holy Spirit, the holy catholic and apostolic Church, the communion of saints, the forgiveness of sins, the resurrection of the body, and the life everlasting. Amen.

Jesus's earliest followers hoped that his death would create the Kingdom of God on earth for both Jew and Gentile. But because his death did not bring about any such major change, his followers set themselves to the task of reinterpreting his message. Some scholars believe that Jesus's intention was to spread Judaism and others believe he did not intend to be literally thought of as the Son of God. But after Jesus's death, his brother James and a follower named Peter insisted Jesus was a king, angering both the Jews and the Romans. The expression *Messianic Hope* is used by both Christians and Jews. Because Christians believe that Jesus is the messiah, the anticipation of his return (Second Coming) is their *Messianic Hope*.

However, for Jews it's different. Jews believe that a great human leader will emerge. Someone like King David. There is a list of tasks that this messiah must accomplish:

The ingathering of the exiles

Restoration of the religious courts of justice

An end of wickedness, sin and heresy

Reward to the righteous

Rebuilding of Jerusalem

Restoration of the line of King David

Restoration of Temple service

(Source: jewfaq.org)

A weakening of Orthodox Judaism (brought about by the Jewish Diaspora) left a void. Christianity filled that void. In the Roman Empire, Jewish Christians, Romans and Greeks, read the new religious writings based upon the teachings of Jesus. They read *the Gospel*. Enthusiastic women helped spread the Gospel and influenced the men in their lives to read and accept the teachings as the new religion.

The Bible was written by about forty different authors. Which means that it has forty different takes on life. In these books, we find law, history, poetry, prophesies, parables and wisdom. The Old Testament was written in the language of the Jews, Hebrew. The New Testament was written in Greek. It requires an open mind to read the Bible objectively. If someone asks you if you believe every word of the Bible, you'd better think twice before answering yes. The good book is full of contradictions, archaic laws and draconian practices. Take from it, the thoughtful, peaceful words of wisdom that speak to you. Leave the rest to history.

Quote
Baptism (Gr. baptizein, to dip in water). Rite of initiation into the Christian Church. As such, it is administered only once, on which point Roman and Eastern and Anglican

churches are all agreed, its validity depending on the pouring of water and use of the proper form of words. Among the Easterns baptism is by triple immersion. The custom of bathing the body in water, to symbolize moral and spiritual cleansing, and to mark initiation at birth or at adolescence into a community, was widespread; but the Church took it over directly from Judaism, where proselytes from paganism were bathed before admission to the community. The method seems to have been immersion, and it was accompanied by instruction in the tenets of the new religion. John the Baptist made baptism a feature of his revival movement, by insisting that even Jews should be baptized in order to prepare themselves for the coming Messianic order. Grolier Encyclopedia Volumes 3&4, pg 56

I can't tell you how many times people have told me that the Bible is nothing but a fairy tale and that Jesus may be fictional. Christians sometimes ponder that question. What if everything Christians are taught is a fairy tale? Many are not dissuaded. Nor were King Henry XIII's subjects back in the 1500's. He had to order all the churches in his kingdom to chain their Bibles to a desk because people were stealing them. In 1537, Bibles were costly. During the 1200's the price for building two arches of the London Bridge was $125.00. The cost for a copy of the Bible was $150.00.

But what does this have to do with genealogy? There are people in the genealogical world who claim that they can trace their lineage back to the *Holy Family*. If Jesus lived to have a family, could someone legitimately trace that far back? I stumbled across the most elaborate family tree I think I've ever seen. It traces back to Charlemagne and then goes even further and links to the Holy Family. Yes... *that* Holy Family, the one that Jesus, Mary and Joseph belong to. I must admit, I'm skeptical. But I also must admit, it is very intriguing. *It could happen.* But did it?

Jesus's mother was Mary. Mary's husband was Joseph. Like Jesus, Joseph was a carpenter. He was a descendant of King David. Descendants are known as being *Davidic*. Recorded in the Old Testament is the Jewish belief that a king of the Davidic line (Royal House of David) would deliver Israel from oppression. A family that for centuries continues the name David in all its various forms may be historically preserving their descent from the House of David. Similar names include: Davidson, Dovid, Davids, Davi, Davis,

Daves, Davin, Davins, Davala, Daviu, Davies, Daud, Daud Ibn, Davila, Davilla and Davision.

Fact or fiction, I do not know but here's the intriguing story: Jesus did not die on the cross. Pontius Pilatus was bribed to spare his life. Jesus was nailed to a cross (the crucifixion) but Pontius Pilatus had him taken down after nine hours, along with the other two men who were crucified along with him. Adherents to this theory say that early Biblical text states that Jesus *suffered* on the cross. Years later, it was edited to Jesus "died" on the cross.

To have children, Jesus needed a woman. That woman (the theory goes) was Mary Magdalene. Mary of Magdala is mentioned in the New Testament for the evil spirits drawn from her and for tending to Jesus's needs. Let's separate Mary from Magdalene. Magdalene refers to Magdala, a location on the Sea of Galilee. She was *Mary of Magdala*. Who was this special Mary who was present at Jesus's crucifixion AND the one who saw him **after** the Resurrection?

The above story is reasoned through Biblical interpretation. I have a friend who is a theologian. He told me that today's rabbis say that the Biblical translation from Hebrew to Greek (called the *Septuagint*) was "one of the greatest tragedies ever to befall the Jewish people." Over two-hundred years before the Christian era, Egyptian king Ptolemy II coaxed enslaved Jews to translate the Bible (the Old Testament). The king promised that their reward for doing so, would give thousands of Jewish slaves their freedom. Jewish scholars wanted to free the slaves. But they had a problem. Jewish law forbade the sharing of the sacred scriptures with those outside Judaism. The punishment for that was death. The Jewish translators got around this quandary by taking sections and incorrectly translating them, most notably Genesis and Ezekiel. My friend tells me that this is why Genesis is inconsistent.

What about the New Testament? My friend told me that "the Apostles and their disciples sometimes refused the Septuagint version. When it differed from the Hebrew, they did their own new translation."

My theologian friend also knows quite a bit about the same conspiracy that Brown wrote about in his, *Da Vinci Code*. Although not a fan of Dan Brown, my friend tells me that the first Christian church was the only one for a long time.

The Holy Family was at the head of the church and their heirs continued heading it. They were the original bishops of the "mother" church in Jerusalem. Around one-hundred-and-thirty-two years after Christ, the *Bar Kochba* persecution of Jewish Christians drove the Holy Family underground. For a few years, there was a revolt. After that, the Romans couldn't tell Jews from Christians, so prohibited both groups from Jerusalem. One-hundred-and-eighty-three years later, the heirs of the Holy Family sought their Jerusalem bishop's seat back. According to my friend, the "paganized Roman church rejected them, and they were then hunted down and killed one by one, except for two people..."

The Da Vinci Code gets a lot of criticism for its inaccuracies. But one thing the book did was stimulate an interest in the idea that Jesus had a family. Many of us would like to see the complete list of the Holy Family members and one cannot help but ask. Am I related?

Quote:
"The Story of Jesus ben Joseph Jesus (Joshua) was the son of Joseph, a member of the Jewish royal family. His genealogy can be traced in the Gospel of St. Luke… He was born in 7BC about 'Easter', rather earlier than he should

have, because orthodox Jews of the time married at 36 & so the earliest proper date of Jesus' birth can be computed as June 7BC. However, Joseph & Mary (Miriam) 'jumped the gun' & one can only approve, as it shows that it was a love match. They had several other sons & two complications now arise in the politics of Judaism: - (1) because the new head of the family was either the first-born Jesus or the unquestionably legitimately- born James. (2) because there was a split in the church between those on the 'right' who wanted to keep Judaism for the Jews and those on the 'left' who wanted to share the religion they thought was a good thing, with the gentiles. Jesus was on the left & James on the right… The Herods, a remarkably smart bunch, juggled this explosive mixture, both temporal - the Jewish Resistance versus the Romans and spiritual - the Jesus faction versus the James one, with considerable skill. As a good orthodox Jew (whether the deeply anti-Semitic Catholic church likes it or not), Jesus married at 36, in 29AD, to Mary Magdalene, a person that Bible-bashers always have a problem with & they had some children… Meanwhile, the story of Jesus' resurrection was spreading… so Jesus himself had to keep his head down. He dictated the Gospel of John to Mark, as with his injured hands, he could no longer write... he refers to himself as 'The Word'… 'Acts' suggests that Jesus was in Rome at the time of Nero's persecution of the Christians but out of the hands of the authorities. He would have been an old man of about 74 at the time. The credibility of the Merovingian connection relies on Jesus' family fleeing persecution in the only direction likely not to be heavily policed - away from Palestine, up Italy & into Gaul. Whether Jesus ever realized that, rather than just spreading Judaism, he had created a new religion, is moot." Pg. 233, The Delaforce Family History Research by Patrick Delaforce and Ken Baldry, 1980-2006.

On January 31st, 2009, I was listening to an early morning show, "God Talk" on KGO radio out of San Francisco. The host of the show, Brent Walters is a professor of religion at San Jose State University in Northern California. He owns one of America's largest private collections of religious books and papers, with some of the earliest Biblical sources ever discovered. His library takes up the whole downstairs of a huge house built during the Gold Rush. It is used by both scholars and students. Although Brent attended a seminary, he became a professor but always felt like, "They are still not telling me something."

Here are some notes I took from the early morning show:

Early Jews Christians: Fast two times a week. Daily prayers. Give alms.

Prayers performed while standing. Jews worked 6 days a week then had Shabbat. Paul called Sunday 8th day of week.

Jewish Shabbat: met early in mornings. Everyone equally shared the responsibility, gathered in homes.

Ruled as a group. Early Christians had no hierarchy. Early Christians had no tithing, just collected alms for the poor.

In the year 321 Emperor created 1st public day of rest. "Venerable day of the Sun." New decree – Sabbatical Law become more and more restrictive.

In the year 585 "Council of Macon" Transfer Sabbath to Sunday. Lord's Day replaced the Sabbath. Council of Churches "Christians must not act as Jews by not working on the Sabbath." In other words, the beginning of anti-Semitism, the transference from the Sabbath to "The Lords Day."

The Jews and Early Christians debated and discussed.

The original [new] testament was in Greek NOT Latin. The Latin is actually a translation of the Greek. The Latin version was poorly translated. There were too many "versions" in Latin. Ecclesiastical Latin is what the Latin of the Bible began to be called and a whole culture developed around it.

The Catholic Church did not stem directly with Paul or the Apostles. The Apostles were ALL married.

Jesus said that he would make it simple enough that a child could understand it.

Peter DID NOT found the Church of Rome. Catholics say this but it's NOT TRUE.

Lots of Jews around the Black Sea.

"The Rock" has nothing to do with Peter, that's just a Latin mistranslation.

The Bible [New Testament] was NOT written in Aramaic, it was written in Greek, and not the common kind of Greek, there were two kinds of Greek.

If you don't understand Judaism, you'll never understand early Christianity. Study the Talmud.

Peter is the most out-spoken and also makes the most mistakes. Catholics call him St Peter.

Jesus was kind of like a big brother to Peter. He would chastise him one moment, praise him the next. Jesus was a Jew. All the Apostles were Jews.

There was an argument as to whether or not to allow Gentiles.

The "Rock" was a confession in faith. Jesus is the rock if there is any not Peter. Peter goes to Rome in chains not as a leader.

The Catholic Church historian who worked for Constantine in 325 AD is the one who wrote that Peter is the founder of the Church of Rome, so it's not based on scriptural truth. It does though become tradition and dogma and legend now. Peter was NOT the Pope and it's false for Catholics to claim this.

End "God Talk" Notes

Interesting Websites

A partial list of Jews who were kicked out of Spain by the inquisition, 5520 names:
http://my.ynet.co.il/pic/news/nombres.pdf

Social Acclimatisation of Jews in 18th and 19th Century Devon, by Reverend Dr Bernard Susser,
http://www.jewishgen.org/JCR-uk/susser/acclimatisation.htm

A resource for those researching slavery:
http://unknownnolonger.vahistorical.org/

Afro-Louisiana History and Genealogy 1719-1820,
http://www.ibiblio.org/laslave/

A "rousing" concert in the ancient Sephardic Synagogue in Amsterdam. Entirely lit by candles. It was built several hundred years ago and never "electrified." During WW II the Nazi's somehow missed it and never entered it, so it is entirely intact and original.
http://www.youtube.com/watch_popup?v=H4IF8OmLOMw

https://www.google.com/amp/s/amp.theguardian.com/science/2015/dec/28/origins-of-the-irish-down-to-mass-migration-ancient-dna-confirms

An extensive list of Dutch Jewish surnames:
http://www.dutchjewry.org/genealogy/devries/totaal.shtml

Bibliography

"HITLER IN HOLLYWOOD, Did the studios collaborate?" by David Denby, pg. 75, The New Yorker, Sept. 16, 2013.

"The Delaforce Family History Research," by Patrick Delaforce & Ken Baldry, Regency Press (London & New York) Ltd and Art & Science Ltd 200, 1988.

"The Memoirs of Samuel Esterowicz in collaboration with Pearl Esterowicz Good." Memoirs translated from Russian and edited by Pearl Esterowicz Good.

https://www.theguardian.com/science/2015/dec/28/origins-of-the-irish-down-to-mass-migration-ancient-dna-confirms

"A Traveler's Guide to PIONEER JEWISH CEMETERIES of the CALIFORNIA GOLD RUSH," by Susan Morris, Judah L. Magnes Museum, Berkeley, CA, 1996.

http://www.taiwandna.com/JewishPage.htm

"Historic Jewish cemetery in Caribbean fades away," by Karen Attiah, Associated Press, November 25, 2012, https://www.yahoo.com/news/historic-jewish-cemetery-caribbean-fades-away-185552977.html?ref=gs

"The History of the Negro Church, Documenting the American South:"
http://docsouth.unc.edu/church/woodson/woodson.html

"The History of the Negro Church," by Woodson, Carter Godwin, 1875-1950, University of North Carolina at Chapel Hill, 2000.

http://www.jewsnews.co.il/2013/05/25/are-native-americans-part-of-the-lost-tribes/
"Are Native Americans Part Of The Lost Tribes?" by Eliyokim Cohen, 5/25/2013.

The New Yorker, "Anti-Semite And Jew," by Anne Applebaum, Nov. 11th, 2013, pgs 28-35.

"The Land of Israel: a text-book on the physical and historical geography of the Holy Land," by Robert Laird Stewart, Read Books, 2008.

YubaNet.com, Mar 26, 2015, "Complex genetic ancestry of North and South Americans uncovered, by Oxford University."

http://www.blackwellpublishing.com/pdf/Incas01.pdf

"HISTORY of PLYMOUTH PLANTATION," BY WILLIAM BRADFORD, THE SECOND GOVERNOR OF THE COLONY (Massachusetts) 1606—1646

"Hadassah Examines the Origins of U.S. Cities with Biblical Names," August 9, 1995:
http://www.jta.org/1995/08/09/archive/hadassah-examines-the-origins-of-u-s-cities-with-Biblical-names

https://www.google.com/amp/s/amp.theguardian.com/science/2015/dec/28/origins-of-the-irish-down-to-mass-migration-ancient-dna-confirms

https://www.google.com/amp/www.sfgate.com/entertainment/amp/KGO-GodTalk-earns-Brent-Walters-heretic-label-2325350.php?client=ms-android-verizon https://en.m.wikipedia.org/wiki/The_Protocols_of_the_Elders_of_Zion

Reports on the Discovery of Peru:
https://archive.org/details/reportsondiscov00sancgoog

https://www.quora.com/

http://www.20000-names.com/character_trait_names.htm

"The Jewish Expression," by Judah Goldin, https://books.google.com/books?isbn=0300019750, 1976.

Grolier Encyclopedia volumes 3, 4, 13, 14, 17, 18, Doubleday, Doran and Co., New York, 1956.

Webster's Collegiate Dictionary.

"Square & Compasses," Dr. Daniel Farhey, Jacob Caspi Lodge, Haifa, Israel:
http://web.mit.edu/dryfoo/Masonry/Essays/pythagoras.html

https://www.sott.net/article/263587-DNA-shows-Irish-people-have-more-complex-origins-than-previously-thought

http://www.jewishvirtuallibrary.org/jsource/Judaism/Sephardim.html

http://www.jewfaq.org/m/mashiach.htm

The Bar Kokhba revolt:
https://en.m.wikipedia.org/wiki/Bar_Kokhba_revolt

"The Northern Light," The magazine for Scottish Rite Masons of America, Volume 47, Number Three, "Masons and the Mason Jar," page 16:
https://www.scottishritenmj.org/images/uploads/northern-light-pdf/2016AUG.pdf

Links to the *Secret Genealogy* Series:

Suellen Ocean is the author of ***Secret Genealogy*** - *A How-to for Tracing Ancient Jewish Ancestry*, ***Secret Genealogy II*** - *Uncovering the Jewish Roots of Our Christian Ancestors,* ***Secret Genealogy III*** - *From Jewish Anglo-Saxon Tribes to New France Acadians,* ***Secret Genealogy IV*** - *Native Americans Hidden in Our Family Trees* and ***Secret Genealogy V****- Black, White and Hamite; Ancestors of Color in Our Family Trees.* ***Available here***:

Secret Genealogy: http://www.amazon.com/Secret-Genealogy-Volume-Suellen-Ocean/dp/0965114082

Secret Genealogy II: http://www.amazon.com/Secret-Genealogy-II-Christian-Ancestors/dp/1484053222

Secret Genealogy III: http://www.amazon.com/Secret-Genealogy-III-Jewish-Anglo-Saxon-Acadians/dp/148407579X

Secret Genealogy IV: http://www.amazon.com/Secret-Genealogy-IV-Native-Americans/dp/1500756105

Secret Genealogy V: https://www.amazon.com/Secret-Genealogy-Hamite-Ancestors-Family-ebook/dp/B01HJ622DU

Printed in the USA
CPSIA information can be obtained
at www.ICGtesting.com
LVHW082017050124
767981LV00025B/139